Legendary Warriors

VIKINGS

by Adrienne Lee

Reading Consultant:
Barbara J. Fox
Professor Emerita
North Carolina State University

CAPSTONE PRESS
a capstone imprint

Blazers Books are published by Capstone Press,
1710 Roe Crest Drive, North Mankato, Minnesota 56003
www.capstonepub.com

Library of Congress Cataloging-in-Publication Data
Lee, Adrienne, 1981–
    Vikings / by Adrienne Lee.
    pages cm. — (Blazers books. Legendary warriors)
    Includes index.
    Summary: "Describes the lives of the legendary Viking warriors, including their daily life,
weapons, and fighting techniques"—Provided by publisher.
    ISBN 978-1-4765-3116-8 (library binding)
    ISBN 978-1-4765-3374-2 (ebook pdf)
    1. Vikings—Juvenile literature. I. Title.
    DL66.L44 2014
    948′.022—dc23   2013010449

Editorial Credits
Megan Peterson and Mandy Robbins, editors; Kyle Grenz, designer; Wanda Winch, media researcher;
Jennifer Walker, production specialist

Photo Credits
The Bridgeman Art Library: ©Look and Learn/Private Collection/Pat (Patrick) Nicolle, 8, ©Look
and Learn/Private Collection/Peter Jackson, 20–21, ©Christopher Wood Gallery, London, UK/
Private Collection/Albert Goodwin, 11, UIG/Universal History Archive, 27; Capstone: Ross Watton,
6–7, 12–15, 26 (bottom); Corbis: Bettmann, 25, Blue Lantern Studio, 16, National Geographic Society/
Tom Lovell, 5, Stapleton Collection, 29; Dreamstime: Tatiana Belova, (cover fire); Getty Images, Inc:
DEA/G. Dagli Orti, 28: Library of Congress: Prints and Photographs Division, 26 (top); Newscom:
akg-images/Johann Brandstetter, 19; Shutterstock: 3drenderings, cover, 1 (sword), bigredlynx,
back cover (sword logo), CreativeHQ, cover, 1 (axe), Veronika Kachalkina, cover (Viking); York
Archaeological Trust, 23

Printed in the United States of America in Stevens Point, Wisconsin.
032013   007227WZF13

Table of Contents

THE WORLD OF THE VIKINGS

Long ago, the Vikings were fierce warriors who attacked villages all over Europe. Vikings took whatever they wanted. They killed anyone who got in their way.

The word *Viking* means "someone who comes from a bay."

Vikings lived in northern Europe in an area called Scandinavia. Land owners with the most money were leaders called jarls. Some jarls had warriors who fought for them.

Scandinavia—the part of northern Europe that includes Norway, Denmark, and Sweden

jarl—a powerful Viking leader

IT'S A FACT

Most Vikings were farmers.
The richest Vikings owned
the most land.

Jarls rewarded their fighters with land and money. Over time, there wasn't enough land in Scandinavia to go around. Vikings who wanted wealth raided other villages.

raid—to stage a sudden, surprise attack on a place

LIFE AS A VIKING

Vikings fought during the summer. Some clans battled for land in Scandinavia. Others sailed longships to search for faraway treasure. These Vikings plundered Europe.

clan—a group of people related by a common ancestor
plunder—to steal things by force

When summer was over, Vikings harvested their crops and settled in for the winter.

 IT'S A FACT

A Viking warrior who
had killed many enemies
was held in high honor.

Vikings warriors lived by a code of honor. They had to be loyal to their family and friends.

Some Vikings were buried in their longships.

13

Committing a crime was considered a disgrace to the Vikings. Being fooled by someone in war or business was also a disgrace. To a Viking, causing disgrace to one's family was worse than death.

Vikings went to meetings called Things twice each year. Legal matters were discussed there.

If one Viking killed another, he had to pay a fine to the victim's family. The fine was called a wergeld.

disgrace—something that causes shame or disapproval

The *Havamal* is a book of Viking sayings. The Vikings believed it was written by their god Odin. One of the sayings in the Havamal is, "Cattle die, and kinsmen die, but honor never dies."

A disgraced Viking warrior had to restore his honor. For the Vikings, revenge was the only answer. Vikings who didn't seek revenge were thought to be weak.

revenge—action taken in return for an injury or offense

VIKING WEAPONS AND ARMOR

A sword was a Viking's most prized weapon. Swords had a thin, double-edged blade almost 3 feet (1 meter) long. Some fathers passed their swords down to their sons. Many Vikings were buried with their swords.

IT'S A FACT

Viking helmets did not have horns. Pictures of Viking helmets often show horns, but this is not the way helmets really looked.

A Viking often fought with a sword in one hand and a battle-ax in the other. Vikings also attacked with spears. Spear blades were 18 inches (46 centimeters) long.

Viking warriors did not wear heavy armor into battle. Most Vikings owned an iron helmet. Rich warriors wore chain mail shirts. Poorer Vikings wore leather armor. Many Vikings carried wooden shields into battle.

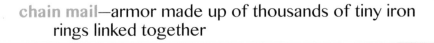

chain mail—armor made up of thousands of tiny iron rings linked together

Armor wouldn't have protected many warriors. A battle-ax could split an iron helmet.

A WAY OF LIFE FADES AWAY

In the mid-800s, a large group of Viking warriors arrived in England. They wanted land. After much fighting, King Alfred the Great finally gave them the northern half of England.

IT'S A FACT

The Vikings' new homeland was called the Danelaw. Vikings also settled in France, Ireland, and Russia.

A Viking named Leif Eriksson was the first European to reach North America. He arrived around the year 1000.

Vikings also sailed far from their homeland. They settled in Iceland, Greenland, and North America. Vikings married local people and became Christians. They left their old ways behind.

Christian—a person who follows a religion based on the teachings of Jesus

In Scandinavia, kings such as Harald Fairhair rose to power. Jarls no longer had control. Clans stopped fighting. By the late 1000s, the Viking culture had faded away. After nearly 300 years, the days of the Vikings were over.

culture—a people's way of life, ideas, art, customs, and traditions

According to stories, King Fairhair didn't cut his hair until he had united all of Norway.

IT'S A FACT

chain mail (CHAYN MAYL)—armor made up of thousands of tiny iron rings linked together

Christian (KRIS-chuhn)—a person who follows a religion based on the teachings of Jesus

clan (KLAN)—a group of people related by a common ancestor

culture (KUHL-chuhr)—a people's way of life, ideas, art, customs, and traditions

disgrace (dis-GRASE)—something that causes shame or disapproval

jarl (YARL)—a powerful Viking leader

plunder (PLUHN-dur)—to steal things by force, often during battle

raid (RAYD)—to stage a sudden, surprise attack on a place

revenge (rih-VENJ)—action taken in return for an injury or offense

Scandinavia (skan-duh-NAY-vee-uh)—the part of northern Europe that includes Norway, Denmark, and Sweden

Corrick, James A. *The Rough, Stormy Age of Vikings: The Disgusting Details about Viking Life.* Disgusting History. Mankato, Minn.: Capstone Press, 2011.

Doeden, Matt. *Weapons of the Vikings.* Weapons of War. Mankato, Minn.: Capstone Press, 2009.

Guillain, Charlotte. *Vikings. Fierce Fighters.* Chicago: Raintree, 2010.

INTERNET SITES

FactHound offers a safe, fun way to find Internet sites related to this book. All of the sites on FactHound have been researched by our staff.

Here's all you do:

Visit *www.facthound.com*

Type in this code: 9781476531168

Super-cool stuff!

Check out projects, games and lots more at
www.capstonekids.com